In the Mynah Bird's Own Words

In the
Mynah Bird's
Own Words

Barbara Tran

Tupelo Press

Dorset, Vermont

In the Mynah Bird's Own Words

Copyright © 2002 Barbara Tran

ISBN 13: 978-0-9710310-5-0
ISBN 10: 0-9710310-5-3

Printed in USA

Third paperback edition, 2007

Tupelo Press
PO Box 539, Dorset, Vermont 05251
802.366.8185 • Fax 802.362.1883
editor@tupelopress.org • web www.tupelopress.org

Cover Painting: *Habitat* by Jeehee Paik
Cover and book design by William Kuch, WK Graphic Design

ACKNOWLEDGMENTS

Antioch Review, *Love and Rice* (Winter 1993)

Arts & Letters Journal of Contemporary Culture
Revelation; Wound, 1968 (published under the title *Wound*); *Fire; Cricket* (Spring 2000)

Asian Avenue, *Faith, Whether in New York or Abilene*
http://www.asianavenue.com/ (Spring 2000)

Asian Pacific American Journal, *Faith, Whether in New York or Abilene* (2000)

Columbia: A Journal of Poetry and Art, *Afterwards* (Spring 1997)

Crab Orchard Review, *Starfish* (Spring/Summer 1998)

CrossXconnect: Writers of the Information Age, *Rosary*
http://ccat.sas.upenn.edu/~xconnect/ (Issue #9) Print version 3.0 (March 1998)

nycBigCityLit.com, *Cricket*
http://www.nycBigCityLit.com/ (September 2001)

Pequod, *Departure's Museum* (Winter 1993)

Ploughshares
Rosary (published as: from *Rosary*) (Spring 1997)

Poetry Nation: North American Anthology of Fusion Poetry
Edited by Regie Cabico, Bob Holman & Todd Swift (Véhicule Press, 1999), *Love and Rice*

Premonitions: The Kaya Anthology of New Asian North American Poetry
Edited by Walter Lew (Kaya Production, 1995) *Fairy Tale; Love and Rice*

Pushcart Prize XXIII, Edited by Bill Henderson (Pushcart Press, 1999)
Rosary (published as: from *Rosary*)

The Southern Poetry Review, *Fairy Tale* (Fall 1992)

Viet Magnet, *Love and Rice* (May 1996)

Viet Nam Forum: Not a War: American Vietnamese Fiction, Poetry, and Essays
Fairy Tale; Love and Rice (Spring 1997)

Watermark: Vietnamese American Poetry and Prose
Edited by Barbara Tran, Monique T. D. Truong and Luu Truong Khoi
(Asian American Writers' Workshop, 1998), *Rosary*

The author extends her deepest gratitude to the Asian American Writers' Workshop, the MacDowell Colony, the Millay Colony, and Tupelo Press.

Thanks also to these fellow writers—and teachers in the truest sense—for their guidance and support in writing... and waiting: Monique T. D. Truong, Tina Chang, Zack Linmark, Bino Realuyo, Tony Gloeggler, Doug Goetsch, Andrea Louie, Christian Langworthy, and Linh Dinh.

Thanks to Jeehee Paik, kindred spirit, for her generosity and extraordinary talent.

Special thanks to Mark Rudman—for starting the fire.

Contents

Long ago, I loved to touch
his long, thin fingers,
his night sky hair,
shiny as mine
but shorter, newer.

My hair, like a net,
captured everyone's interest.
Their words clung to my hair
like barnacles to stone.
The tide could do nothing
to wash the words away.

And my swings
from right to left,
from rosary to whiskey sour,
only made them hold on tighter.
His father was one of the barnacles.
The old man imagined himself combing my hair.

At first, I was his little one,
with knots in my hair
from running wildly
through the rice fields.
He wanted me cross-legged
on his lap.

But the old man combed farther
and farther down.
And my hair
reached my waist
and past.

He jumped off the water buffalo, and I knew we'd be married.
He turned it easily, pushing its head to the side.
The orange *diep* trees were like blazes of sun
hanging in the air below the clouds.

I told Mother that night he was my lover.
He knew nothing of it.
I thought of nothing else as I wrung the sheets.
That he was my cousin didn't matter,
there was no room for shame.
Grandmother would notice the sun setting
and know her clock needed winding,
know she had missed her bananas and rice.

That first time I touched him, I thought of nothing but fruit.
There was no electricity then, night came early.
I took a long bath, pouring water
gently over my body, watching it drip
between the wooden slats.
Soon, I'd be carrying
a weight inside me.

Afterwards

His crib sat in the corner of the room.

He cried but no one responded.

The music came to me

in a symphony of colors, one

on top of another, mutating.

My only explanation came in dreams.

In a knock on the door.

I saw the scythe in his smile.

April brought the sun and his first step.

For a day, I thought perhaps I'd live.

But he fell on his knees, banged

his chin. My son now

is learning to swim.

The boy vanishes in water

like sleep. Then nothing

is heard. Life is a reflection

that ripples with each memory.

The sea is lifted with each kiss.

This boy that cried like a girl

abandoned in the mountains of China.

The snow, an endless blanket.

With his arrival, they called me *darling,*

sweetheart, honey, mother.

I answered to nothing.

Xuong

From outside Church, I could see the priest shielding the candle as he approached the altar with it. I wondered about all the whiteness inside, how the slightest amount of color could pollute it all, something Mother repeated to Sister Eight time and again as they embroidered together. The thread needed to be tested, washed first, before it was drawn into cloth, or it might bleed. She undid the thread from its spool, one loop, two. Any more and it might tangle. She hated waste. I stood there in the mist outside Mass, feeling myself being reeled out. Somewhere inside was the woman who was doing the pulling. Myself, unwound, I waited. There was no turning back, the knot was already there. At the market, I chose a few sweet treats, watched as they wrapped them in newspaper, stretched a bright rubber band around the package. The sweet grease leaked through. I licked it from my fingers. This was how it would feel to kiss her, after.

Wound, 1968

Xuong

In America,   on the TV screen,
images I cannot regard

but imagine   all too clearly
each night:

the trees   bursting with leaves, the boys'
faces beaming with youth,

the light   explosive.
In this portrait of life

in bloom,   red would seem
the color of a flower.

And it blossoms   this way, in the center
of a young girl's

mind,   across the shoulder
of the brother

who tried   to shield her.

Xuong

After the mynah bird's tongue was split open by the chili peppers
he fed it, after the rough outer layer of its tongue peeled off, after it
finally did what he commanded, after the bird gave in and cawed,
Speak, stupid, speak, morning after morning, Uncle Five would have
given anything to return it to its original ignorant state. Instead, day
after day, he was greeted with the same stale command he himself
had issued to the bird. Only then did he recognize his mistake, and
only now, do they recognize theirs. In the eyes of the other men I see
bewilderment that I have been allowed to fly free in their home. *Where
is his cage,* I know they wonder. *Who has let him out?* I long now for
my wife to join me, to feel her body curl into mine, the way certain
words in Vietnamese charm my tongue and settle deep in my chest.

Rosary

Do I begin at the here and now,
or does the story start
with the first time
my mother took the wheel—
the first woman to drive
in a country where men
are afraid to walk?

My mother's story begins
when the steam rises.
It ends when it's ready.
Taste it. Does it need more salt?

Today, at 67, she stands at the stove at work. The heat overcomes her. She thinks she is standing at the shore. The steam is like a warm breeze being carried out to sea. My mother hears the seagulls circling above. She feels the sun on her skin and admires the reflection on all the shining fish bodies. Her father's men have been collecting the nets for days now, laying the fish out for fermenting. The gull with the pure white underside swoops toward the fish farthest away, lands on an overturned boat, its sides beaten and worn, its bottom sunburned like a toddler's face after her first day of work in the rice fields. Beside the boat, a palm hut, where the fishermen hang their shirts, where their wives change when it's time for a break from the scooping and jarring, when their black pants become hot as the sand itself. And then the laughter starts, and the women's bodies uncurl from their stooped positions, their pointed hats falling back, the men treading anxiously in the water as they imagine a ribbon pulling gently at each soft chin.

bait

Through the eye, my grandfather threads the rusty hook, forces it back through the body of the fish. The tail curves around as if frozen mid-leap. The seagulls never leave. The smell of fish always in the air. Today, the old man will give them nothing. It is his daughter he is thinking of. My mother is fourteen and beginning to turn heads. Her father thinks she will like the seagull with the pure white underside. He watches the birds, daring one another to come closer. He watches the younger ones in their confusion. The swoop and retreat. He has not fed them for days. Minutes go by, and he thinks the boats will come in soon, scattering the gulls. The Year of the Snake is only days away. He would buy his daughter a dove, but she likes the wind. With a quick swoop, a gull grabs the fish in its beak. The old man wraps the line around his roughened hands, braces himself for the tug as the line grows more taut. And suddenly the bird jerks in the sky, wings extended as if it's been shot.

She knew it was coming by the way the glass jars shook in the darkness, the occasional flash of lightning, crawling the walls like quick lizards. A rain so heavy, things would be hammered into the earth. She thought of all the glass jars resting on their shelves, all the hours the men spent, blowing these cylinders for the *nuoc mam* they made from the anchovies they caught, and then, the few drinking glasses they made for themselves on the side when her father wasn't watching. After the rain, the broken pieces would once again have to be melted down and mixed together. And here, her father lay in bed, smoking away the profits. With each breath in, the fishing boats moved further and further away. With each breath out, more jars needed to be made, sold. Her father couldn't even hear the thunder. The lightning, warm flashes on his lids, like the sun when he was trying to nap in the afternoon. He thought the glass-blowers earned him a puff on his pipe with each puff on theirs. He should reap the rewards of being an old man, of owning his own fishery. But with each breath, his daughter grows more impossibly beautiful. He knows he will not be able to keep her long.

For years, my grandfather thought he could keep my mother by his side. She seemed content with her prayers and fasting. But he didn't know about the couple that sat before her at Mass that Sunday morning. She had noticed them, the man sitting next to the woman as if she were any other. But then, the stolen glances, the passing of a prayer book, the spreading of goose-bumps, from the neck down the arms, the woman crossing herself.

The first time my father saw my mother, she was driving the barren countryside of Bien Ho. How vain, he thought to himself: wearing Easter lilies in her hair. What he didn't know was that they actually were Easter lilies: she was on her way to Mass. She wore them year-round to remind herself that Jesus was always risen—if you kept Him alive in your life.

They were married before her father knew it,

her father smoking opium in the bright sun.

All he could remember

was the white jacket, the black tie,

the boat rocking, the boys reaching,

dragging the net.

The net full of fish.

The fish drying in the sun.

The seagulls swarming like men

honing in on the scent.

The slow peeling of an orange.

Smoke coming from his pipe.

The juice squirting.

The spewing out of pits.

And then, she was packing.

prayer

My grandfather had always had three women in the kitchen, someone continuously preparing something. Fresh bread, hot banana pudding, sweet rice with coconut. And now his daughter was leaving, and the women were selecting china for her to take. He wondered how this happened. She was the last of his daughters, and he had spoiled her, hoping to keep her for himself. For years, he spent his days, from the moment he woke until the sun began its slow dive into the water, submerged, working the fishing nets, his skin puckered like a mango left in the sun too long. And here, his daughter would still need to watch the gills heave up and down, the gasping at the small mouth. Still, she'd need to chop the head off, blood running down the sides of the cutting board, her hands covered with scales. For years, he tried to keep her hands from coming in contact with anything but the food she ate and the money she counted. Now they would be roasted daily over a fire.

He wondered how crowded her new home would be, how long she would have to live with her in-laws, how such a small child would bear a child. He knew she would find it difficult to breathe in the smog-filled streets of Saigon. He closed the trunk for her, knelt down beside her, pressed a bar of gold into her palm. He wanted her to write as often as possible. She nodded. She wanted to stay, to hold her father's hand, to watch the fishing boats come in, to listen to the seagulls like hungry beggars outside.

hope

It all began with her driving the barren country roads, barren because the men were too fearful to walk them. Knife-blade to the neck, my mother still refused to hand over the pearls her father gave her for her first Christmas as a teen, as a target for unmarried men. Really, what she hoped they wouldn't find was the pearl rosary her mother left behind. She felt the blade bite deeper into her neck: the same place her husband would often bite her the first year they were married, the last year she would think of love as something shared between two people.

In Saigon, a daughter on each hip, she began to wonder where the rice was going. Leaving one child home sucking her thumb, the other holding her empty belly, my mother hailed a taxi. In front of the cathedral, the pink nails in the car ahead crept across the man's neck, and she recognized both. This was, after all, the man who woke her body. Before him, she knew only the ache of chopping and carrying, of balancing heavy loads. Now there was a different kind of pull, like the sea, and after it, a different kind of heavy load, filling her belly. Of course, she followed him.

On the way back from the market each day, the pole teeters across her back, a pot on either side. The one on the right, emptied of its *pho;* the one on the left, full of dirty bowls and the leftover dishwater she was too impatient to drain. Cuong skips ahead, his short hair bouncing with each step. She quickens and grabs her youngest son's ear, twisting it, not because he is getting too far ahead, or because he is daydreaming, but because she can't. Her husband gone with the oldest two children, my mother still has four. He lives in a duplex in Manhattan; she sells *pho* for ten cents a bowl and needs someone to hold. Cuong is getting too big, with his slingshots and firecrackers, his patched eye from Tet. Each day she drags my grandmother's bed a little closer to hers, brings a mirror along with dinner to her mother's bedside.

My mother's recipes are not even close to precise. Everything is in approximate proportion. One portion of *nuoc mam* to three of water and one of vinegar, some lime, a big pour of sugar. Maybe some more. This is in opposition to her determination to keep my father. With this, she was painfully methodical.

Brush stroke number forty-nine
and her hair shines like a black cat's.
She can think of nothing
but the days when she wore her hair
above her shoulders, moved her hips
like a boy. And still the men
couldn't help but look. Now
there are so many things
to fit into the frying pan:
the daughter with the red
lingerie rolled inside her dirty
school uniform, the son
with the twisted jaw
and a constant longing
for cold beer, the husband
she chased in taxicabs,
holding her extended belly
only to finally say, *Please,*
take me home. At seventeen,
my mother counted her Hail Marys
on the little white beads
of her rosary. Now she counts them off
on the heads of her seven children,
counting herself as eight,
and her husband,
as one and ten.

This would have no meaning without a lie or two,
so I'll bend a few lines, call it your benefit.
The truth is not always very instructive.

The other night, the moon rose, orange and full,
over Brooklyn. The woman beside me,
the one from out of town,

thought it a particularly good
view of New York. I didn't have the heart
to tell her

it wasn't New York, but a postcard, a lie
of the magnitude that holds this city
together. Instead I told myself

to remember this:
the way the moon rose,
larger and rounder

than the wide mouth
of the cup the man held
as he danced to no music,

the woman whose scarf
led her
from one end of the pier

to the other, in search of someone

who could help her hear

what wasn't there.

I told myself

if I could paint this picture

in words, that someone

would recall it the way I didn't,

someone

put the orange back in the moon.

Someone

would keep the river flowing,

someone

fill the ferry with mad revelers,

someone slip change

in the runaway's pocket.

And someone

would make sure

the woman was there

the next morning

to meet her lover

in Abilene.

Departure's Museum

All around lie the scars:
under my hand, behind his lowered hat,
at the bottom of a bottle.
Oblivious, the stewardess continues
to serve coffee. Cream
swirls in; the movie plays on.
Where is the snow
here replaced by the fluff of clouds?
My glands now swell with the plague
of his muddy waters
and loud winds, our smoke-
filled rooms and his stacked boxes.
The myth of a tethered dog's
master returning.
The myth of a home.
The myth of ice. The months
proceed always in the same order.
Photographs are the only record
of the death of a day.
He dies over and over in my memory.
I refuse to buy film.
A headache is proof enough.
You can see through ice:

Look, the sandbars are frozen.
The fish swim in deeper waters.
They die with a hook through the gills.

When I heard *courtyard,*
I thought: light, gardens, mansion.
I don't need to tell you
it wasn't that way,
the courtyard simply a shaft
bringing no light
to the two floors.
The second floor was theirs,
the GIs my mother rented the place to.
Now she sees it is small and dank
and cannot imagine not stealing
the GIs' coffee and canned soup,
not taking a quick
four-finger swipe

of peanut butter.
If my mother were telling this story,
you'd hear of the servants,
of my oldest sister's
unbroken yolks,
perfect parts and even braids,
my second sister's
clown and pony parties.
Remember where we are—
my oldest brother
who didn't learn to walk
until he was five.
Notice, though, the other children
—there are three of them—

are not mentioned.

Notice, their voices

no longer sing, but shout.

Notice the youngest,

dragging himself across the floor.

Notice his brother,

sitting on a potty

in the corner,

shitting worms.

Notice their sister

grasping a rat-tailed comb

by its teeth.

At night I lie
close to my husband
hoping to camouflage myself
against his body
as if when he is dreaming
he might mistake me
for a cricket
on the blade
of his back.
Cricket and blade together
sway
in the wind,
thin as a breath,
both rooted to the land.

I dream of being alone
in this field.

It has been years
since I have been able
to be with my husband
at his whim.
And now I carry
another wish—
the result of the banishment
of our children to their room.
Alone with me,

he has nothing
to say and so
must touch.
We will have seven
come this August.

She was an after-

thought in every conversation.
They acknowledged her by erasing her.
Who would want to be stuck
discussing her, or worse,
conversing with her? They—
and she grew to believe them—
thought that it would be best
to forget her rather than have her
be the disappointing focus
of conversation.

In shadow, she could be a sensation:
a dancer, a surgeon, a natural
at soccer. She learned to dodge
the limelight, jump to its side
even when it tailed her. The applause
never gave her pause; she knew
it wasn't meant for her. In shadow,
she learned to steal

the goods, how to drop a word or two here
and there, slip them into the conversation,
so that fifteen minutes later,
all would turn around and wonder
how, during discussions of vacation,

they ended up agreeing

to have dinner in a greasy diner.

She began to view this as a gift:

her ability to escape notice. She could sit

right next to them, cough during the opera,

but somehow, they'd look around

without suspecting her. Her reputation

began to precede her.

They anticipated her arrival at every

press-covered event. They searched

the crowds with a spotlight. Photographers

roved the streets surrounding. Gossipers

sat silent, hoping to catch her in the act,

but they couldn't keep still long enough.

Somehow she slipped in

while they were whispering

and was gone

before they could ensnare her. The crowd

was searched for witnesses, but everyone

shrugged their shoulders: not one

insightful word

could be said   about her.